Handwriting workbook for kids

This book belongs to

_____

Available now on Amazon

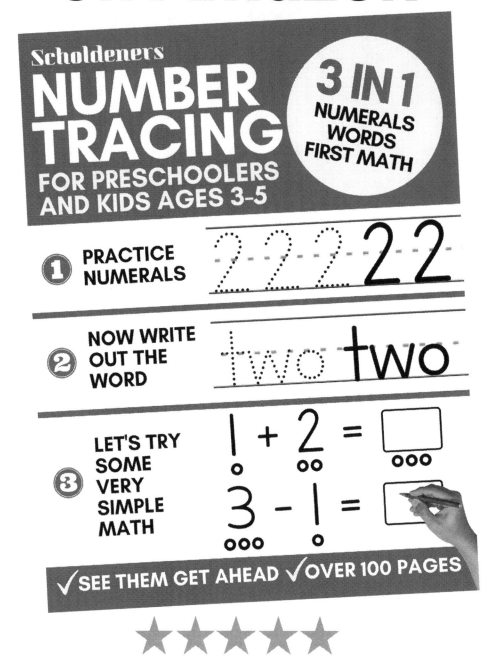

Get Ahead Quickly in Numeracy

- 110 pages – with more than 100 pages of writing exercises
- This 3-in-1 workbook will gently guide the child from beginner until they are happy and confidently writing numbers, spelling them out and doing basic fun math

Introduction & Tips

Learning handwriting is a key milestone in a child's academic journey. This is an exciting time, but can also be a little daunting for the child. To make learning as smooth and effective as possible, here are ten top tips:

1. Body basics
Good posture is important for cursive writing. Encourage children to sit with their feet flat on the floor, their back straight (no heads on the table) and relaxed shoulders.

2. Think Ink
Although children usually write in pencil at school, it can be useful for them to start cursive handwriting with felt tips and gel pens, which have a nice, fluid delivery of ink.

3. B prepared
If your child is using a pencil, the softer B pencils are generally easier to write with as they move more fluently across the page.

4. Let loose
Don't stick to practising on paper. Get children to practise their letters in other mediums, such as tracing them in the air, in sand with a stick or on another person's back with their finger. Make learning fun and creative.

5. Get a grip
Keep an eye on the child's pencil grip. It's important that the pad of the thumb connects with the pencil. If the side or tip of the thumb touches, it closes up the hand and restricts the flow of movement.

6. Let's twist

The child may find cursive writing easier if their paper is at an angle. You can turn the page up to 45 degrees in either direction.

7. Left learning

Left-handed children may have more trouble as they push the pencil across the paper, rather than pulling it. A writing slope can be beneficial for left-handed children as it helps them to see their writing.

8. Teaching terms

To help your child at home, ask how handwriting is being taught at school: for example, do they refer to entry and exit strokes, flicks or tails? It's important to use consistent language so you can give your child effective instructions.

9. Method matching

Handwriting styles vary from school to school, so it's important to be consistent and ask children to write 'f's, 'r's, 'k's and other letters that tend to vary in style the same way at home and in the classroom.

10. Easy does it

Finally, keep handwriting practice light and fun. Nagging your child about their writing will only reduce their enthusiasm. Always give praise where it's due and try not to hover over them - they need time to fully experience each task.

Part I: Learning letters

Trace the dotted letters on the top line, then write the letters in the remaining space

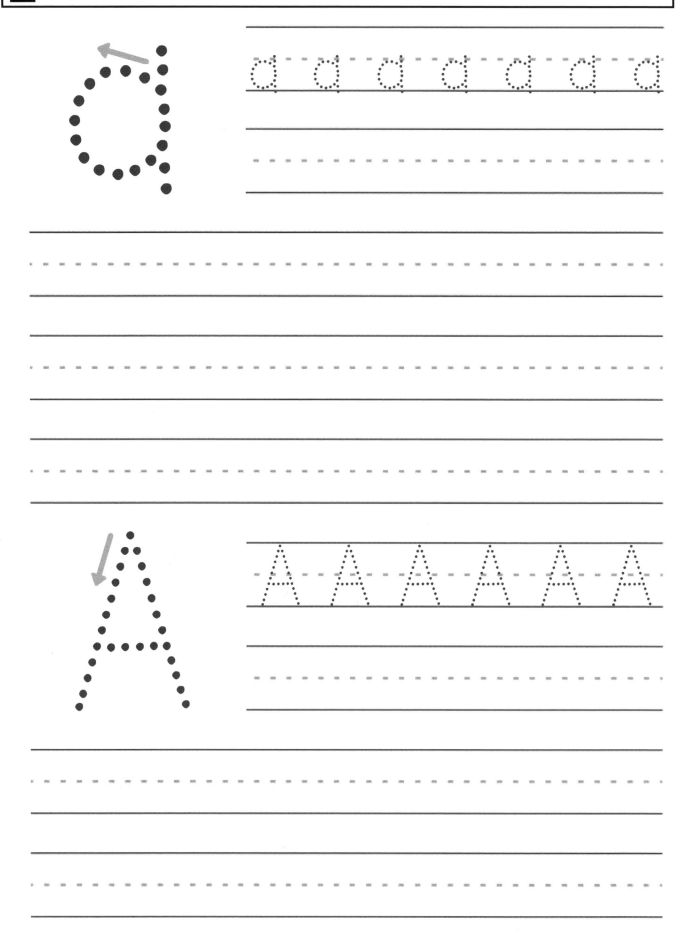

A B C D E F G H I J K L M N O P Q R S T U V W X Y Z

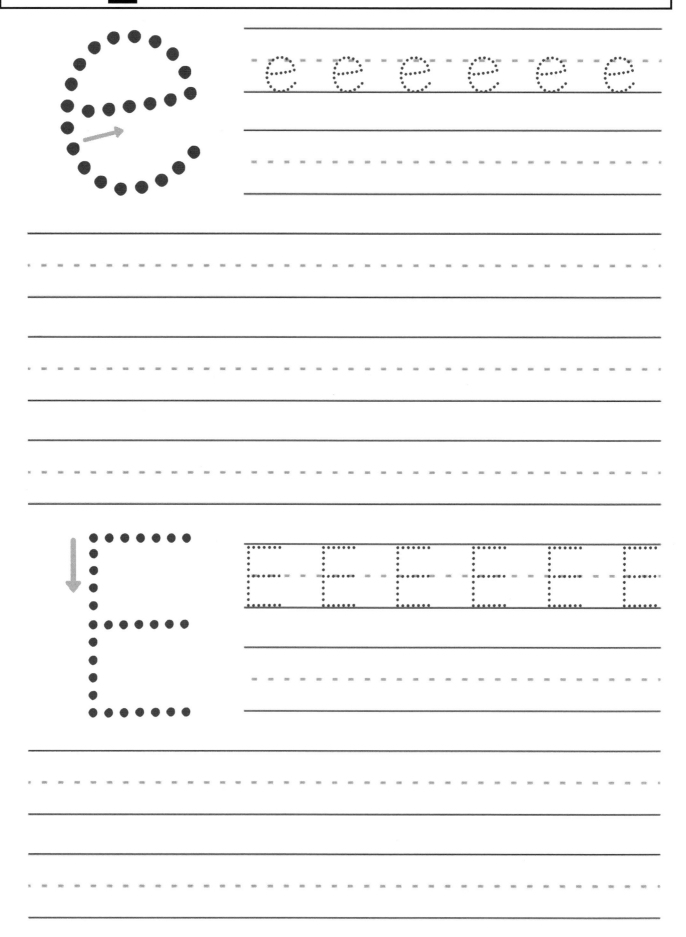

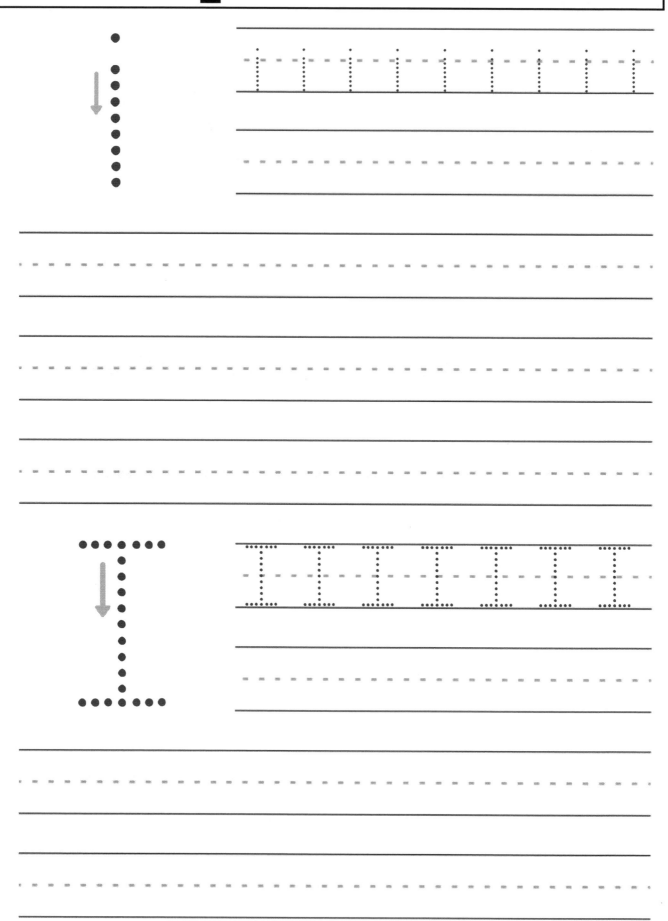

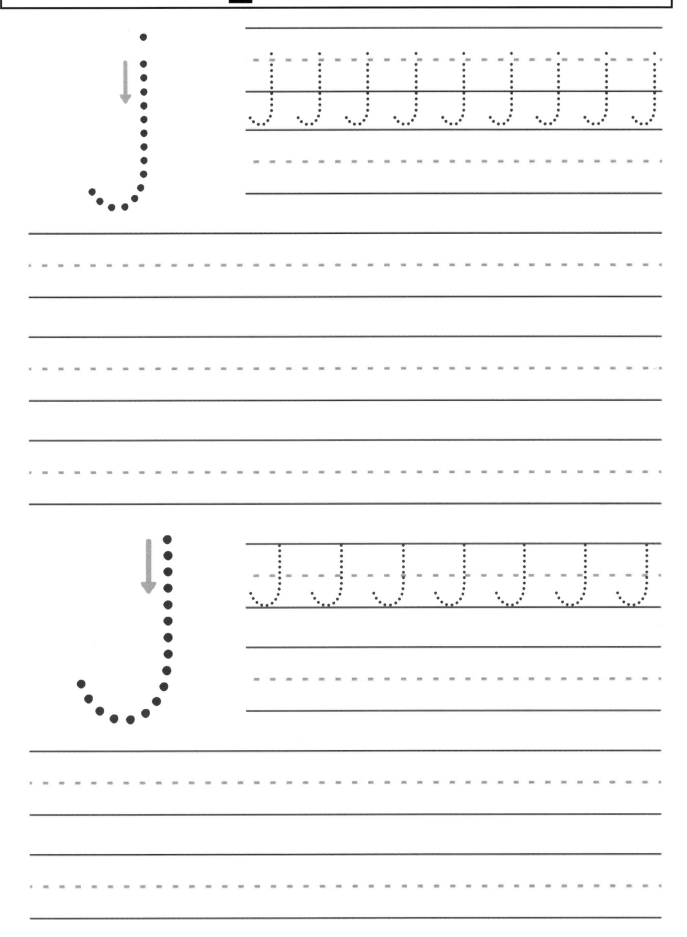

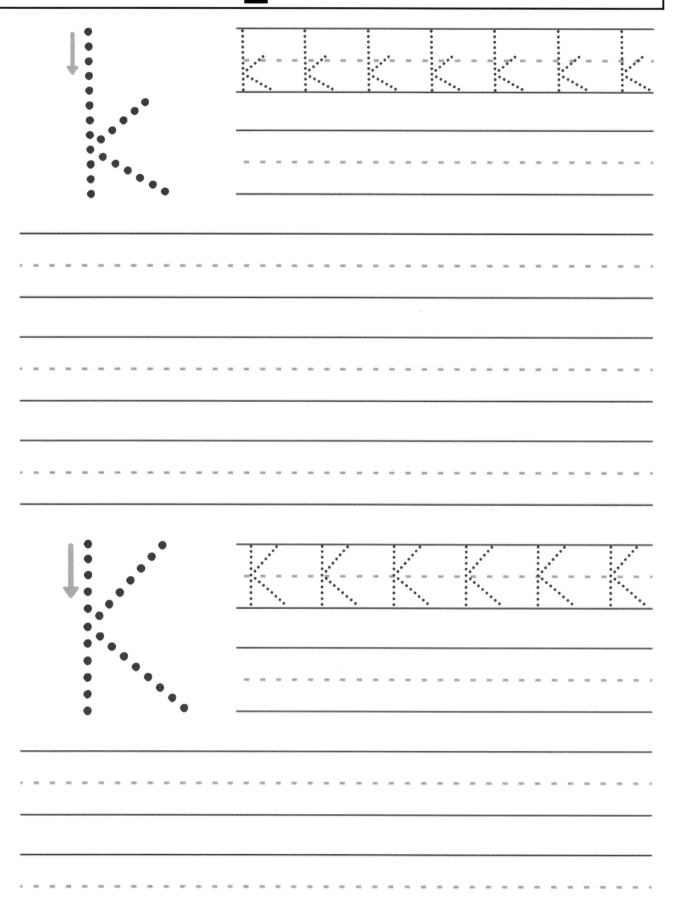

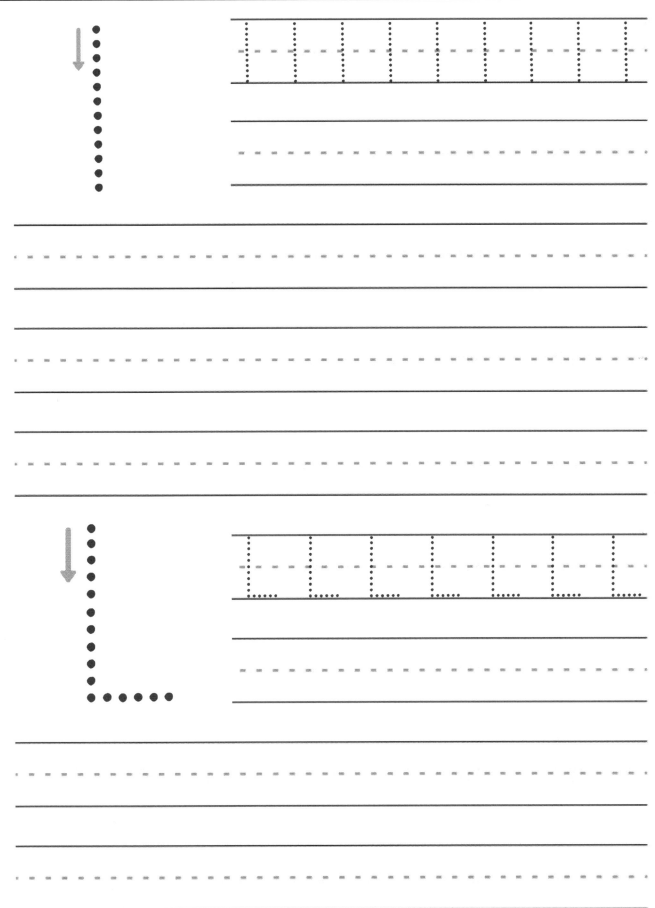

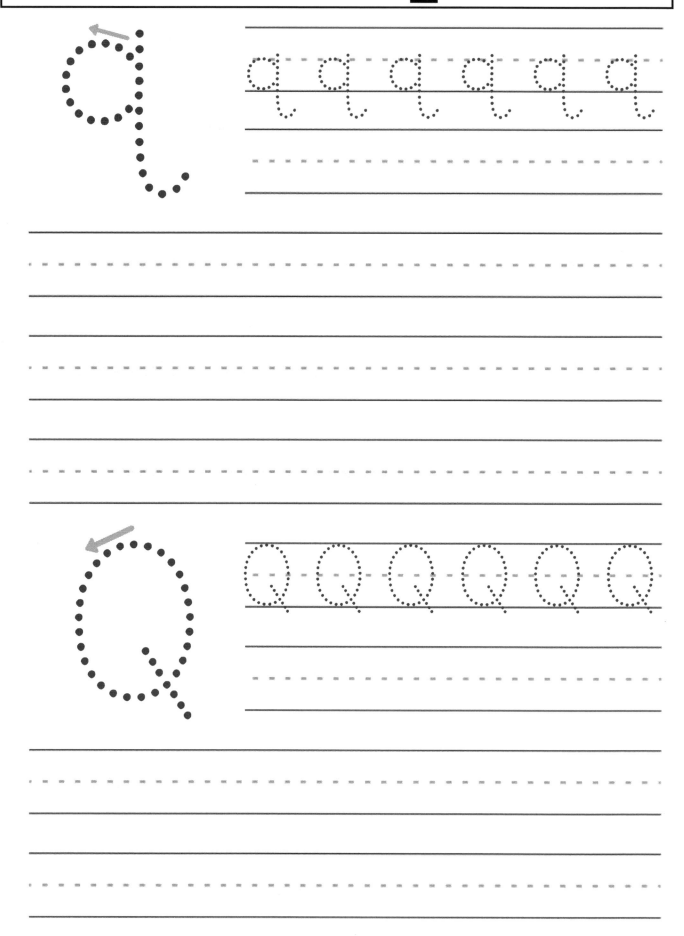

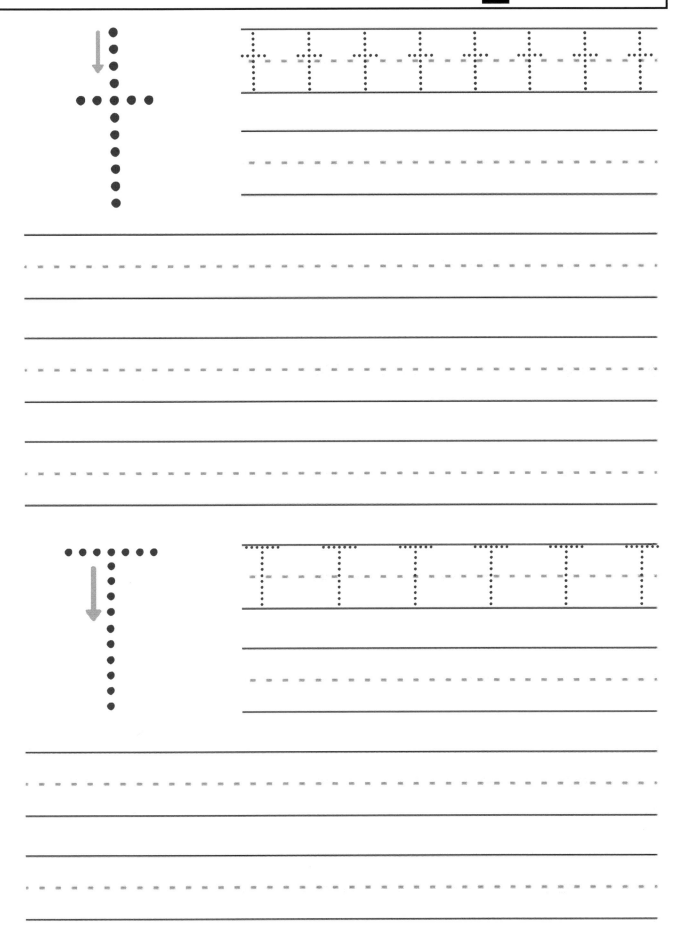

A B C D E F G H I J K L M N O P Q R S T U V W X Y Z

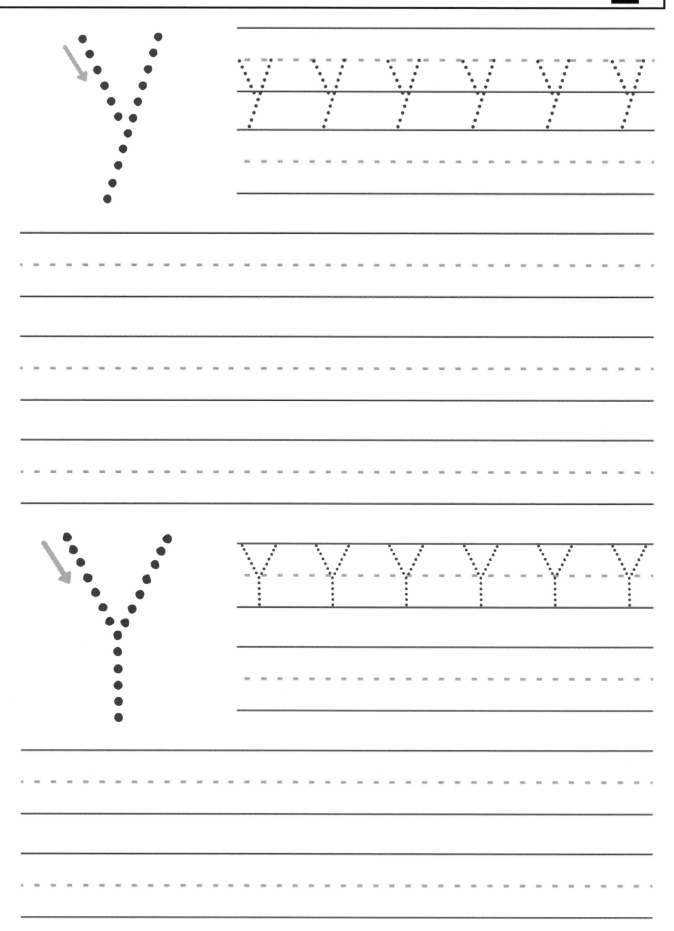

Part 2: Simple Words

Trace the dotted words on the top line, then write them in the remaining space

(By the way, you're doing brilliantly!)

boy boy boy boy

What do you call a dinosaur that is sleeping?

girl girl girl girl girl

A dino-snore

baby baby baby baby

Why did the teddy bear say no to dessert?

food food food food

Because she was stuffed

moon moon moon

What did one plate say to the other plate?

hand hand hand

Dinner is on me

glad glad glad glad

Why did the student eat his homework?

name name name

Because the teacher said it was a piece of cake

pony   pony   pony

Why did the kid cross the playground?

truck truck truck

To get to the other slide

late late late late

Why was 6 afraid of 7?

wind wind wind

Because 7, 8, 9

nice nice nice nice

What kind of tree fits in your hand?

doll doll doll doll

A palm tree

candy candy candy

Why did the cookie go to the hospital?

use use use use use

Because he felt crummy

your your your your

Why was the baby strawberry crying?

away away away

Because her mom and dad were in a jam

best best best best

lunch lunch lunch

What did the little corn say to the mama corn?

Where is pop corn?

club club club club

What falls in winter but never gets hurt?

what what what

Snow

drive drive drive

How do we know that the ocean is friendly?

very very very very

It waves

each each each

tree tree tree tree

How does a scientist freshen her breath?

With experi-mints

farm farm farm

soon soon soon soon

How can you tell a vampire has a cold?

He starts coffin

goat goat goat goat

How do you make an octopus laugh?

riding riding riding

above above above

What did the nose say to the finger?

become become

Quit picking on me

cattle cattle cattle

Why couldn't the pony sing a lullaby?

dinner dinner dinner

She was a little hoarse

everyone everyone

Why didn't the skeleton go to the dance?

family family family

He had no body to dance with

ground ground ground

Why did the banana go to the doctor?

heard heard heard

Because it wasn't peeling well

inches inches inches

What do you call a funny mountain?

Juice Juice Juice

Hill-arious

Kitten Kitten Kitten

Why do bees have sticky hair?

Large Large Large

Because they use a honeycomb

Merry Merry Merry

Why did Johnny throw the clock out of the window?

noise noise noise

Because he wanted to see time fly

Orange Orange

What do you call an old snowman?

Picture Picture

Water

Queen Queen Queen

What time should you go to the dentist?

Running Running

Tooth hurty

Shield Shield Shield

Why did they quit giving tests at the zoo?

Teacher Teacher

Because it was full of cheetahs

Under Under Under

What room can no one enter?

Value Value Value

A mushroom

Winter Winter Winter

Why couldn't the pirate learn the alphabet?

Xray Xray Xray

Because he was always lost at C

Zapping Zapping

yesterday yesterday

What are the strongest days of the week?

Saturday and Sunday. Every other day is a weekday

remember remember

What goes tick-tock and woof-woof?

everybody everybody

A watchdog

Literacy Literacy

What do monsters turn on in the summer?

astronaut astronaut

Their scare conditioner

Different Different

Why do shoemakers go to heaven?

Suddenly Suddenly

Because the have good soles

President President

Want me to tell you a joke about pizza?

Sentence Sentence

Sorry, it is too cheesy

probably probably

important important

Why was the broom late?

It overswept

happiness happiness

favorite favorite

Why did the golfer wear two pairs of pants?

In case he got a hole in one

Countries Countries

What word starts with E and has only one letter in it?

Beautiful Beautiful

Envelope

attention attention

What do you give a sick lemon?

transform transform

Lemon aid

ambition ambition

What animal is best at hitting a ball?

ingenious ingenious

A bat

medicine medicine

What did the blanket say to the bed?

maximum maximum

I've got you covered

Encounter Encounter

What kind of snack do you have during a scary movie?

Dominate Dominate

Ice cream

I am great at writing

Why do tigers have stripes?

Bring on part three!

So they don't get spotted

Part 3: Sentences

Carefully read the joke
or riddle, then write
it in the space below

(Has anyone told you you're
amazing at handwriting?
Well you are!)

What do you call it when a dinosaur crashes his car?

Tyrannosaurus Wrecks

What gets wetter and wetter the more they dry?

Towels

What is big, green and plays a lot of tricks?

Prank-enstein

What are full of holes but still hold water?

Sponges

Why does the
sun have to
go to school?

To get brighter

Where do cows go for some entertainment?

The mooooo-vies

Who is the person that everyone has to take his hat off too?

_____

- - - - - - - - - - - - - - - -

_____

- - - - - - - - - - - - - - - -

_____

- - - - - - - - - - - - - - - -

_____

- - - - - - - - - - - - - - - -

_____

The barber

_____

- - - - - - - - - - - - - - - -

_____

What creatures are smarter than talking parrots?

Spelling bees

What never asks questions but is often answered?

_____

- - - - - - - - - - - - - - - -

_____

- - - - - - - - - - - - - - - -

_____

- - - - - - - - - - - - - - - -

_____

- - - - - - - - - - - - - - - -

_____

Doorbells

_____

- - - - - - - - - - - - - - - -

_____

What's the worst thing about throwing a party in space?

_____

- -

_____

- -

_____

_____

- -

_____

_____

- -

_____

You have to planet

_____

- -

_____

What belongs to you but other people use it more than you?

_____

- - - - - - - - - - - - - - - - - - -

_____

- - - - - - - - - - - - - - - - - - -

_____

- - - - - - - - - - - - - - - - - - -

_____

- - - - - - - - - - - - - - - - - - -

_____

Your name

_____

- - - - - - - - - - - - - - - - - - -

_____

What was the snake's favorite subject at school?

_____
- - - - - - - - - - - - - - - - -
_____

_____
- - - - - - - - - - - - - - - - -
_____

_____
- - - - - - - - - - - - - - - - -
_____

_____
- - - - - - - - - - - - - - - - -
_____

Hisssstory

_____
- - - - - - - - - - - - - - - - -
_____

What word becomes shorter when you add two letters to it?

_____

- - - - - - - - - - - - - - -

_____

- - - - - - - - - - - - - - -

_____

- - - - - - - - - - - - - - -

_____

- - - - - - - - - - - - - - -

_____

Short

_____

- - - - - - - - - - - - - - -

_____

What did the pencil say to the other pencil?

You're looking sharp

What has to be broken before you can use them?

_____

- - - - - - - - - - - - - - - - - -

_____

- - - - - - - - - - - - - - - - - -

_____

_____

- - - - - - - - - - - - - - - - - -

_____

_____

- - - - - - - - - - - - - - - - - -

_____

Eggs

_____

- - - - - - - - - - - - - - - - - -

_____

What is the best day of the week to go to the beach?

Sunday

Where does Friday come before Thursday?

In the dictionary

Why should you always take a pencil to bed?

To draw the curtains

What is so delicate that saying its name breaks it?

_____

· - · - · - · - · - · - · - · - · - · - · - · - · - · - · -

_____

· - · - · - · - · - · - · - · - · - · - · - · - · - · - · -

_____

_____

· - · - · - · - · - · - · - · - · - · - · - · - · - · - · -

_____

_____

· - · - · - · - · - · - · - · - · - · - · - · - · - · - · -

_____

Silence

_____

· - · - · - · - · - · - · - · - · - · - · - · - · - · - · -

_____

What do you call a bear with no socks on?

_____

- - - - - - - - - - - - - - - - - -

_____

- - - - - - - - - - - - - - - - - -

_____

- - - - - - - - - - - - - - - - - -

_____

- - - - - - - - - - - - - - - - - -

_____

Bare-foot

_____

- - - - - - - - - - - - - - - - - -

_____

What did the beach say when the tide came in?

Long time, no sea

What is the best thing to do if a bull charges you?

_____

- -

_____

_____

- -

_____

_____

- -

_____

_____

- -

_____

Pay the bull

_____

- -

_____

What is an astronaut's favorite place on a computer?

The space bar

Why did the bumble bee put honey under his pillow?

To have sweet dreams

What is something you will never see again?

Yesterday

What did the outlaw get when he stole a calendar?

Twelve months

What are two things you cannot have for breakfast?

Lunch and dinner

What did one potato chip say to the other?

_____

. . . .

_____

_____

. . . .

_____

_____

. . . .

_____

. . . .

_____

Shall we go for a dip?

_____

. . . .

_____

Can you guess what is at the end of a rainbow?

The letter W

Why did the boy bury his flashlight?

The batteries died

What type of cheese is made backwards?

Edam

Why do birds fly south in the winter?

It's too far to walk

If two's company and three's a crowd, what are four and five?

Nine

What did the little tree say to the big tree?

Leaf me alone

What did the tree wear to the pool party?

Swimming trunks

Who deserves a huge treat for mastering handwriting?

_____

· ·

_____

_____

· ·

_____

_____

· ·

_____

_____

· ·

_____

You do!

_____

· ·

_____

That's it!

You have done fantastically well!

Now keep it up and take your handwriting to the next level.